INDO- U.S. DEFENCE COOPERATION

INDO- U.S. DEFENCE COOPERATION

By

Gp Capt (Retd) GD Sharma, VSM

Centre for Joint Warfare Studies (CENJOWS), New Delhi

Vij Books India Pvt Ltd
New Delhi (India)

Published by

Vij Books India Pvt Ltd
(Publishers, Distributors & Importers)
2/19, Ansari Road, Darya Ganj
New Delhi - 110002
Phones: 91-11-43596460, 91-11- 47340674
Fax: 91-11-47340674
e-mail : vijbooks@rediffmail.com
web: www.vijbooks.com

Copyright 2013 © Centre for Joint Warfare Studies, New Delhi

ISBN: 978-93-81411-43-8

All rights reserved

No part of this book may be reproduced, stored in a retrieval system, transmitted or utilised in any form or by any means, electronic, mechanical, photocopying, recording or otherwise, without the prior permission of the copyright owner. Application for such permission should be addressed to the publisher.

The views expressed in the book are of the author and not necessarily those of the Centre for Joint Warfare Studies, New Delhi/ publishers.

Contents

Foreword   ix

Preface   xi

Historical Perspective	1
Moving Forward, A Strategic Compulsion	8
Geo-Political & Economic Realities	16
Building of Defence Partenership	21
Current Status of Partenership	28
Challenges Ahead	46

Foreword

Today India and the U.S. share a convergence of interests on many fronts. This has been ushered due to the rapid pace of changes in the Indo-Pacific region and the consequent shift in geo-political and geo-economic centre of gravity. The countries have initiated dialogue and cooperation on strategic issues, in counter-terrorism; information exchange, defence etc. Considerable mutual trust has been built up and continues to move beyond the period of decades of geopolitical alienation. Two way trade in goods and services is growing in a balanced manner and may touch US$ 100 billion this year. The non existent defence trade has also increased and United States is the third largest weapon supplier with current orders worth US$ 8 billion on US equipment manufacturers. Defence Services, once unfamiliar with each other now hold regular dialogue and joint exercises. India does more joint exercises now with the U.S. armed forces than with any other country. Defence cooperation incorporating a strong component of joint production, research and co-development is also visualised, a vision which hopefully U.S. Government shares.

Many in India tend to view United States with as much suspicion as China despite Beijing's role in bolstering our hostile neighbour's missile and nuclear weapon programme and continual claim on Indian territory. Generational change in India is producing an increasingly young, globalized middle class which aspires to see India as one of the great power. They are more comfortable with projection of liberal idea of India which is closer to the United States.

Of late, Americans are criticising India for carrying opportunistic trade with Iran despite Western sanctions. Iran is the second largest crude oil supplier to India after Saudi Arabia. It is neither easy nor right to stop oil trade with Iran as sanctions are outside of the United Nations umbrella. In a fiercely competitive market there is no reason to believe that Saudi Arabia may not exploit any monopoly position in India's energy import basket. India's foreign policy believes in "Strategic Autonomy" hence, it will never be the kind of pliant "ally". Both India and the U.S. need each other to be strong partners - for their own betterment.

Gp Capt (Retd) GD Sharma, VSM, Senior Fellow of this centre in his study titled "Indo-U.S. Defence Cooperation" has traced the Indo U.S defence relations from the past when their policies and other differences in world view became a major barrier in developing close military relationship to the present strategic partnership. He has also deliberated on the challenges and way ahead to overcome these.

(KB Kapoor)
Maj Gen(Retd)
Director, CENJOWS

Preface

In the Asian century, India faces complex existing and emerging strategic challenges in the region. In that, the threat from Pakistan and China looms large and therefore, occupy the minds of the Indian strategic thinkers and defence planners. Despite pacifying changes in Pakistan's, it is still ridden by unstable internal polity, its nuclear safety concerns and military linkage and sponsorship of the terror groups, as well as Pakistan's Chinese linkage which foretells their designs against India. In that, Chinese ominous presence in POK needs a special mention. At the same time, Chinese military modernisation and infrastructure development in southern Tibet cast evil shadows its Northern and Eastern borders of India. What is of specific concern to India is that china's infrastructure build up in terms of roads, railway network and airports etc indicates its capability and readiness without having to physically deploy forces. This infrastructure development may also be due Chinese new military doctrine i.e., waging short wars under conditions of informationisation. From east to west directions of the Yarlung Tsangpo River the highway is ready. With that, the Chinese capability to induct troops from Eastern China has significantly risen. Hence, in real terms, the threat from china has increased many folds. The developing strategic situation is being dealt both at diplomatic as well as at the Military level. In that United States is playing pacifying and stabilising role.

While we look forward to better relations with both Pakistan and China but, this can only be achieved from the position of strength. While Chinese are being matched to some extent by force developments in the north-eastern provinces but this is not enough. The potent counterbalance capabilities alone can help in bridge long- and short-term differences with the intransigence neighbours. Defence cooperation with America which has been the leader of scientific research and technological innovations is important to India because of lack its own adequate defence Industry and Technology. In the recent times, United States has emerged as one of the three largest arms exporter to India. More significantly, India's increased purchase of arms from the US has gone hand in hand with increased Indo-US defence cooperation. Since the beginning of rapprochement, in the past 16 years, India and the US have signed several defence cooperation agreements, and conducted several joint military exercises more than any other country which signifies growing Indo-U.S. defence cooperation.

- GD Sharma
Gp Capt (Retd)
Senior Fellow, CENJOWS

Historical Perspective

Historically, America remained largely indifferent to India's freedom struggle. Thereafter, after the Second World War, the US policy of containment of communism and India's policy of nonalignment became major irritants in relations. After emerging from colonialism and external domination, India's immediate concern was to assert its independence. India thus sought to take independent positions on international issues without being tied down by alliances and ideological constraints. Over time, other countries also decided to remain "non-aligned" with India emerging as a prominent leader of the nonalignment movement. On global issues, non-alignment was often seen as aligning against the west. This policy therefore precluded the possibility of a military relationship with any country or grouping. This policy and other differences in world view became a major barrier to an Indo-US military relationship throughout the Cold War.

Paradoxically, later circumstances brought the democratic India closer to erstwhile communist Soviet Union with whom it even signed the peace and friendship treaty in 1971 and continues to maintain close relations even now while the democratic America veered closer to authoritarian Pakistani regime. It even drafted Pakistan in SEATO and CENTO cold war groupings to counter expansion of communist regimes. Thereafter, Indo American relations have always seen through the Pakistani prism. The Indo–Soviet Peace and Friendship treaty was a significant deviation from India's position of non-alignment. The treaty in its original form was not renewed. After disintegration of Soviet Union, India has entered in to Treaty of Friendship and Cooperation with Russia in 1993 but, it does not have security clauses of the earlier treaty which called for active security support to each other.[1]

---

[1] Russia & India .Report August 9 ,2011. Toasting Legacy of 1971 Indo –Soviet Friendship Treaty by .Arun Mohanty.http://indrus.in/articles/2011/08/09/toasting_ legacy_of_1971_indo-soviet_friendship_treaty_12842.html

India US relations got strategic content in early 1960. Chinese annexation of Tibet, its role in the Korean War and other such acts convinced Washington about the expansionist designs of the Chinese. But this was short lived as during the cold war there was a definitive pro Pak shift for the reason as brought out above.

Early Indo- U.S. Defence Relations

Defence Relations after India's Independence. After India's independence, United States considered Pakistan an important ally strategically to contain the Soviet expansion in Asia. Its location closer to the Soviet empire endowed it with a special geo-strategic advantage. The West could not ignore the potential benefits provided by Pakistan. The impact of U.S. policy was immediately felt in the case of Jammu and Kashmir (J&K). India got a rude shock after it took the case of Pakistan's aggression of 1948 in J&K to the United Nations with the expectation that Pakistani aggression would quickly be recognized and steps taken to vacate the state of Pakistani forces. UN Commission on India and Pakistan instead asked India and Pakistan for cessation of hostilities, Pakistan to withdraw its troops and tribal forces while asking Indian government to maintain bare minimum troops for general administration of the area. The withdrawal of troops was never carried out by Pakistan which was a pre-condition for Plebiscite agreed by both India and Pakistan.[2] India was thus confronted with the realities of emerging geo-politics.

An attempt at forging military ties between India and the United States was first made soon after Indian independence in the late 1940s by Indian Defence Attaches, first Colonel Brij Mohan Kaul and later Brigadier Dilip Chaudhuri. Kaul requested the US Defence Secretary, Louis Johnson, to sell forty three B-25 bombers and a wide range of weaponry to New Delhi. Chaudhuri followed up these discussions with a request for tank ammunition too.

---

[2] UN Resolution 47 21 Apr 1948, The UN Security Council after hearing complaint of India and reply and counter complaint of Pakistan set up a UN commission of five members to decide the accession of Jammu and Kashmir to India and Pakistan which recommended free and impartial Plebiscite to decide whether state of J&K will accede to India or Pakistan. http://www.un.org/documents/sc/res/1948/scres48.htm

The proposals did not find favour with the US administration and relations with India were restricted to sharing limited and low grade military information. The considered view of the US government was that India was not a region of strategic interest to the United States. Nevertheless, a modest beginning was made at this time. The United States was still the first country to provide military aid to India after its independence. It approved the sale of 200 Sherman tanks for $19 million, although it rejected another request for 200 fighter aircraft. It questioned justification for making such defence expenditure when India was taking huge development aid from the United States. Later, rebuffing Pakistan's claim that any arms supply would alter the military balance in the region, the US government supplied 54 C-119 Fairchild military transport aircraft to India.[3]

The next brief historic interlude in India–US military exchange was the role played by Indian forces in the repatriation of prisoners of war in Korea in 1953. The actual task of prisoner repatriation was carried out by a six thousand strong Indian contingent under General Thimayya. Ambassador Arthur Dean of the United States expressed his "tremendous appreciation" for Thimayya and the Indian contingent for "a most amazing job in extremely difficult circumstances".[4]

Pakistan joined the US-led military alliances SEATO and CENTO. US had sought India to join but in accordance to avowed policy of non-alliance India refused to join these groupings. In fact, Ayub Khan even gave U.S. an air base near Peshawar from where it operated U-2 spy planes to spy Soviet union in the thick of the cold War. India just would not have accepted this.

Indo-U.S. Defence Relations in Sixties

The relations between India and China deteriorated in late fifties. What is notable was the dramatic shift in Indian policy and the generous military and political support that India received from the United States and the West.

---

[3] An article "Indo- Us defence and Military relationship from Estrangement to Strategic partnership" by Dipankar Banerjee in book ,US Indian Strategic Cooperation in to the twenty-first century edited by Sumit Ganguly , Brian Shoup and Andrew scobell.

[4] Ibid

None of India's non-aligned partners provided help and few showed any sympathy. Moscow actually temporarily halted the MiG programme, siding instead with its socialist brother, China. Due to various reasons, however, the ultimate quantity of aid was not as high as initially expected in India and did not, therefore, have a lasting impact. The supplies were restricted to light arms, automatic weapons, and winter clothing and communication equipment sufficient for little more than one infantry division. But, this alliance was short lived as America did not see any advantage in continuing this relationship. While it was known even at the time of the 1962 war that Nehru had sought 'general' help from the US, the extent to which Nehru had gone in seeking military aid was not known. However, recently disclosed letters by JF Kennedy library, Nehru sought military aid from the US in the form of air power including fighter aircraft and pilots to handle them and train Indian staff. Nehru went on to specifically ask for 12 squadrons of supersonic all-weather fighters, two squadrons of B-47 bombers and a modern radar system. He also mentioned that these aircraft would have to be manned by US personnel while the Indians were still being trained. But as we know now US did not accede to Indian request.

The given aid in fact consisted of innocuous non-lethal hardware. Curiously, under US advice, Nehru was deterred from using the Indian air force. Though small no doubt, it could still be expected to decisively interdict the PLA advance from the many air strips in eastern India. By comparison, even though China had a larger inventory of aircraft, these were old and could have even carried very limited pay loads while operating from high altitude airfields in Tibet. A considerably larger arms package of US $373 million was apparently worked out by November 1963 in Washington by Ambassador Chester Bowles and was to have been signed by President Kennedy on November 26, 1963, but it did not materialise due to untimely death of the young President.

Later Lyndon Johnson and India's differing views on the Vietnam War precluded any possibility of fostering any close relationship between the two countries. Nevertheless, though inconclusive and limited, this engagement ultimately proved to be a high point of Indo-US defence cooperation in sixties.

During 1965 India Pakistan war, United States cut off sales of weapons to both India and Pakistan. It was also stung with developing close relations between China and Pakistan. As disclosed in US declassified documents, the Johnson administration was troubled by signs of this close and highly secret cooperation between China and Pakistan. But, it did not translate in developing close relations with India. Johnson Administration suspected that Pakistan had even started maintaining distance from U.S. Vietnam policy to please China. Both Pakistan and China had highly tense relations with India which was central to their close cooperation, but this did not make the Johnson administration sympathetic to India.[5]

India Pakistan War 1971

The pro Pak bias was once again evident in India Pakistan war of 1971. The USS Enterprise which had sailed past in show of US support of India in 1962 India China War, once again sailed from Hawaii to the Bay of Bengal, but this time against India. The declassified documents show that US ordered stoppage of two million dollars of arms supplies and delay in signing of food aid programme PL-480 and development loan to pressurize India to back off from then East Pakistan.[6] This correlates with narrative given in MEA file noting, "On December 1, 1971, the U.S. government also announced its decisions against India to suspend issuance of future munitions list licences, not to issue any new licences or to renew existing ones. While announcing the decision, the U.S. government informed us that this did not affect outstanding licences for Indian scheduled purchases in the US which were valued at approximately $11.5 million," but in two days a nasty surprise was yet in store for India. The MEA file notes "Two days later, the US government also announced the suspension of these licences" too.[7]

Declassified top secret papers on the 1971 war show that, US hostility towards India during our war with Pakistan was far more intense than known until then. The papers disclose that, Nixon Administration had kept three battalions of Marines on standby to deter India, and that the American aircraft carrier USS Enterprise had orders to target Indian Army facilities.

---

[5] US State Departments declassified transcripts India-Pak War '1971 : Note from Thomas Hughes, Director of Intelligence and Research, U.S. Department of State, to Director of Central Intelligence, W.F. Raborn, 21 July 1965, enclosing paper on U.S.-Pakistan policy problems, Secret Source: U.S. National Archives, CIA Research Tool (CREST)

[6] Ibid

[7] An article in 06 Nov 11 Times of India based on declassified documents by Josey Joseph

Disclosures also bring out that during 1971 United States continued to supply arms to Pakistan despite taking a stand to maintain equidistance from both. On June 22, 1971, the New York Times reported that Pakistani ships loaded with US arms headed for the Pakistan coast despite a US embargo on arms supplies to both Islamabad and New Delhi.

As though this was not enough even in United Nations, the American delegation accused India of aggression. In the Security Council and the General Assembly they tried to mobilize support in favour of Pakistan. The US introduced a ceasefire resolution in the UN Security Council on Dec 4, but it was vetoed by Soviet Union. It is during this time India signed a treaty of friendship which was offered for a long time by the Soviets. India was worried by the Chinese intervention but, after the treaty, Brezhnev ordered 40 Soviet Divisions for deployment against China border kept the Chinese intervention at the check. US even tried to persuade China to open a new war front against India and assured its support in case of a retaliatory attack on China. As china refused to oblige, President Nixon ordered a Carrier Task Force of the US seventh fleet, led by USS Enterprise, in to Bay of Bengal. Soviet Union responded by dispatching two carrier groups of Cruisers and Destroyer from its Pacific fleet and a submarine armed with nuclear missiles from Vladivostok. On 12 Dec 71, the Chinese formally conveyed their stand on the crises and decided not to open a front in India's Northeast much to the chagrin of Pakistan.

US maintained its aggressive posture throughout seventies. US Air Force carried out aggressive surveillance sorties from America's newly-acquired Indian Ocean base of Diego Garcia and Thailand which kept getting more and more frequent and hostile through the seventies and provoking Indian vessels.[8]

One can assess the extent of opposition of United States to India for it not only branded India as an aggressor for the 1971 war in the Security Council but, as the recent revelation from the archives show that even contemplated military intervention. On December 14, Gen A A K Niazi, Pakistan's military commander of erstwhile East Pakistan had told the

---

[8] Times of India, 06 Nov 11. An article based on declassified documents by Josey Joseph http://articles.timesofindia.indiatimes.com/2011-11-09/india/30377450_1_defence-secretary-indian-navy-foreign-secretary

American consul-general in Dhaka that he was willing to surrender. The message was relayed to Washington, but it took the U.S. 19 hours to relay it to New Delhi. Files suggest senior Indian diplomats suspected the delay was because Washington was possibly contemplating military action against India.

Pokhran I: India's Peaceful Nuclear Explosion 1974.

India's decision not to participate in the Nuclear Non-Proliferation Treaty (NPT) in the 1970s and later Peaceful Nuclear Explosion (PNE) of 1974 brought a further low in the Indo-US relations. The Nixon Administration had given low priority to India in its foreign policy. The White House was focused on the Vietnam War and grand strategy toward Beijing and Moscow. Intelligence on nuclear proliferation was a low priority hence, India's "peaceful nuclear explosion" on 18 May 1974 caught the United States by surprise. International reaction to the Indian blast was mixed. The Non-Aligned Movement member states applauded India's technological breakthrough. France in fact sent congratulatory messages to the Indian Atomic Energy Commission. The United States however, imposed restrictions to limit India's access to nuclear material and technology. The test focused the international attention to proliferation, and overseas support for India's nuclear programme disappeared. Canada in fact, cut off all nuclear assistance after the test, bringing two nuclear power projects -Rajasthan II reactor and the Kota heavy water plant - to a halt. Indeed the nuclear non-proliferation regime that exists today came about as a direct result of this test.[9]

United States and other NPT countries for nearly three decades, imposed sanctions on India for developing a nuclear weapons programme outside the NPT regime. It resulted in India's isolation from the rest of the world on all nuclear issues. The events from sixties till eighties show that United States and India remained on opposite sides during the Cold War .Even as the Cold War came to an end, Washington focused on deepening its alliances with Europe and Japan and engaging a rising China and India was kept off the list of U.S. foreign policy priorities.

---

[9] http://www.globalresearch.ca/index.php?context=va&aid=28066

Moving Forward: A Strategic Compulsion

At the end of the cold war with the demise of the Soviet Union, India had to adapt to the new reality of the uni-polar world. Some 70 percent of aircraft and their parts and a high portion of other military hardware were sourced from the USSR. Not only did New Delhi require a new source for military hardware, but reliance on the Russia for a whole range of diplomatic support was no longer possible. It was clear that the global order would be recast and old ideological impulses reviewed. India had to adapt to this new reality.[1]

In July 1989 Shri K.C. Pant visited the United States, the first by a Defence Minister in twenty-five years. He went with a delegation that included all three Vice Chiefs of Staff of the Indian armed forces, the defence secretary and the Scientific Adviser. In the United States, he announced a semi-official strategic dialogue between the Institute of Defence Studies and Analyses (IDSA), New Delhi and the Institute of National Strategic Studies, National Defence University, Washington, DC.

Indo-US defence and military ties got further impetus in 1991 after the visit to India by Lieutenant-General Claude M. Kicklighter, Commander-in-Chief, U.S. Army Pacific Command. His proposals, subsequent to his dialogue with then Maj Gen Rodrigues, included service-to-service exchanges and expansion of a defence cooperation framework. Indeed this was the beginning of structured military-to-military cooperation between the two

---

[1] An Article titled,'an overview of the Indo-US strategic Cooperation: A roller coaster relationship. By Dipankar Banerjee in US-Indian Strategic Co-operation in to the 21st century- More than words..edited by Sumit Ganguly, Brian Shoup and Andrew Scobell

countries. Executive Steering Groups (ESGs) were established in both countries to intensify military-to-military cooperation. An Army ESG was set up in January 1992, followed by formation of Navy and Air Force ESG in March 1992 and August 1993 respectively.

Track 2 Initiatives

A series of strategic dialogues, first held at Washington in September 1989 thereafter were convened semi-annually. These meetings were the near equivalent of Track 2 dialogues, with the difference that over half the participants were senior government officials attending in their personal capacities so that they articulate their views fairly freely and frankly and feel out the other side's interests and concerns. Participants included ambassadors, senior military officers, civilian members of government from the foreign and defence ministries, and leading strategic experts.

The second round of strategic dialogue took place in November 1990 at the National Defence Academy, Khadakwasla. It was perhaps also the most successful round of talks. The comments of the Director, Institute for National Strategic Studies (INSS) who were co-sponsor of the meeting summed up," he felt like some one who had been witnessing the family reconciliation after long period of estrangement". The meeting was attended by a number of U.S. officials, including the U.S. Ambassador to India, William Clark. The Indian side was represented by the Chairman Chiefs of Staff, senior officials from the Ministry of Defence and External Affairs, and senior Strategic Analysts.[2]

The next meeting was held in July 1992 at the Airlie House in Virginia, Washington. This conference too was a success. Assistant Under-Secretary of State, Teresita Schaeffer led the US delegation, which consisted of officials from the Departments of State and Defence as well as senior analysts from major think tanks. The Indian delegation comprising Indian Ambassador Abid Hussain, Rear Admiral Sushil Kumar, later the Chief of the Navy and Chairman Chiefs of Staff Committee was led by Defence Secretary N.N. Vohra. The Admiral proposed the *Malabar* series of joint naval exercises

---

[2] Ibid

off the West coast of India in Autumn of 1992, the first such joint exercises to be undertaken by the Indian armed forces with the United States.

The next meeting at Jaipur in 1994 was less successful. It did seem that the novelty of this exercise was perhaps beginning to wear off and each side was repeating the issues and hoping for a break-through where perhaps none was possible.[3]

"Agreed Minutes" of Defence Relations 1995

The US Defence Secretary William Perry who visited India in January 1995 took Kicklighter-Rodrigues initiated defence cooperation process forward. He signed an "Agreed Minute" outlining Indo-US defence cooperation with his counterpart in India, Shri Mallikarjun, then Minister of State for Defence. Under this agreement, a Defence Policy Group and a Joint Technology Group were established, which provided for greater interaction between civilians, scientists and the militaries of both sides. In the meetings that followed, several strategic issues were identified by the two sides: stability of the West, Central and South West Asian states, oil security in the Gulf, future internal dynamics in China, South East Asia, the Indian Ocean area, and international terrorism.[4]

However, despite the signing of these Agreed Minutes, there were differences in the perceptions on the agreement between the two countries. Perry stressed the fact that sale of arms or transfer of technology or even joint technology development was not part of the Agreed Minutes. **Firstly**, this was simply an agreement to strengthen bilateral cooperation gradually, particularly in the field of defence research and production. **Secondly**, no arms/technology transfer would be done at the expense of Pakistan. Pakistan thus remained a significant factor in any US dealings with India.[5]

---

[3] Ibid

[4] An Article titled,' Indo-US Defense and Military Relations: From Estarngement to Strategic Partnership. By VP Malik in US-Indian Strategic Co-operation in to the 21st century- More than words edited by Sumit Ganguly,Brian Shoup and Andrew Scobell

[5] Ibid

Impact of Pokhran II on Defence Relations

On 11-13 May 1998, India carried out five nuclear tests in the Rajasthan Western desert, 24 years after the first test in 1974. This invoked strong condemnations and sanctions from several developed countries including the United States. Japan, the only state which had suffered the U.S. nuclear bombing in 1945 was the first state to take punitive action against India .Germany, Sweden and Denmark followed the suit .But what seemed to escape that India had neither violated any agreement nor broke any international laws, but merely attempted to safeguard its own national interests in a manner that it considered appropriate.

As expected United States imposed sanctions as required by its domestic law (Glen Amendment to the nuclear non-proliferation act of 1994, applicable to the non-nuclear nations as per their status in 1967), on May 13, 1998 President Clinton signed the Presidential Determination No. 98-22, a memorandum for the Secretary of State, in accordance with section 102 (b) (1) of the Arms Export Control Act, imposing economic sanctions on India. Section 102 of the Arms Export Control Act, as amended (Glenn Amendment), prohibits a variety of assistance and commercial transactions between the United States and any other country if the President determines that the country (a non-nuclear weapon state), detonated a nuclear device. Under President's written determination, the following were affected:

(a) Termination of US assistance under the Foreign Assistance Act of 1961: food or other agricultural commodities except for humanitarian assistance;

(b) Termination of US government sales of defence articles, defence services, design and construction services, and licenses for exportation of US Munitions List items;

(c) Termination of foreign military financing under the Arms Export Control Act;

(d) Denial of any credit, credit guarantee, or other financial assistance by any department, agency, or instrumentality of the US government, excluding those related to humanitarian assistance or congressional oversight of intelligence activities;

(e) Opposition to the extension of any loan or financial or technical assistance by any international financial institution (IFI), in accordance with section 701 of the International Financial Institutions Act;

(f) Prohibition on any US bank from making loans or providing credit to the governments of India or Pakistan, excluding loans or credits to purchase food, or other agricultural commodities;

(g) Prohibition on exports of "specific goods and technology," excluding food, agricultural commodities, or items related to congressional oversight of intelligence activities, in accordance with section 6 of the Export Administration Act of 1979, relating to foreign policy controls.

However, many of these sanctions were removed through Congress–Executive decisions between 1998–2000, as follows:

(a) On July 14, 1998, the House of Representatives voted to lift some sanctions related to agricultural credits and on July 16, 1998 Congress passed "The India-Pakistan Relief Act of 1998," sponsored by Senator Sam Brownback (also known as the Brownback I). Brownback I allowed the President to waive the application of sanctions provided in sections 101 and 102 of the Arms Export Control Act, *with the exception of (B), (C), and (G) of section 102 pertaining to military assistance, arms sales, and sensitive technologies exports.*

(b) On October 21, 1998, the Congress authorized removal of sanctions against India and Pakistan in the Brownback amendment to the FY 99 Omnibus Appropriations Act (HR 4328)13. The bill gave President the authority to waive most of the sanctions and resume finance and other assistance programs up to one year.

(c) In November 1998, President Clinton, exercising his waiver authority vested under Brownback I, restored some non-military aid programs in India and lifted restrictions on the activities of U.S. banks in India.

(d) Another amendment in October 1999 waived sanctions on

environmental programmes and other activities. But it maintained sanctions on programmes affected by:

(I)   Prohibition of Foreign Assistance Act (FAA)-funded activities

(II)   Prohibition of Foreign Military Sales (FMS)

(III)   Foreign Military Financing (FMF), and

(IV)   Prohibition of licenses for export of items on the US Munitions List, certain dual-use exports, and for certain end-users. The amendment also gave President the authority to prune the list of Indian entities placed under restriction.[6]

The remaining sanctions were removed just before President Obama's visit of India in Nov 2010. The sanctions by U.S. and other sanction regimes viz Nuclear Supplier Group, MTCR, Australian Wassener group brought in after 1974 and 1998 nuclear tests seriously delayed India's progress but also benefited by building self reliance in space, nuclear and missile technologies.

It is now well known that PM Vajpayee explained to the U.S. President the compulsion and rationale for the nuclear tests in which he pointed clearly to China as the principal security concern of India and barely four months later Prime Minister Vajpayee declared in a speech at New York that India and the United States were "natural allies."[7] Other Group 8 nations (seven developed nations and Russia) did not follow the U.S. They however regretted India's action and hoped to negotiate and get India to sign the CTBT as way to lift the sanctions. India on its part also showed its willingness to negotiate and even declared unilateral moratorium on further nuclear tests[8].

---

[6] Ibid

[7] An Article titled,'an overview of the Indo-US strategic Cooperation: A roller coaster relationship. By Dipankar Banerjee in US-Indian Strategic Co-operation in to the 21st century- More than words..edited by Sumit Ganguly,Brian Shoup and Andrew Scobell

[8] http://www.iwar.org.uk/news-archive/crs/6202.pdf

Consequent to the tests, the Security Council adopted a resolution 1172 (1998) strongly condemning the nuclear tests. India of course in response brought out the duplicity of the world body that it had not taken cognisance of the many hundreds of nuclear tests carried out over the last 50 years, including in 1995 and 1996, when the de facto moratorium on testing, was already in place[9].

Jaswant Singh-Strobe Talbot Strategic Dialogue

When the Cold War ended and all other irritants largely vanished, nuclear proliferation remained the only issue between India and the United States. Ironically, this single agenda brought India and U.S. together. After India's May 1998 nuclear tests, then Deputy Secretary of State Strobe Talbot engaged India's then foreign minister, Jaswant Singh, in 14 rounds of talks over two and a half years which truly was the first sustained strategic engagement with the Indian leadership. By February 1999, around mid-way into the talks, the United States felt that it had achieved a fair degree of success, making India agree to sign the CTBT as well as be a party to the FMCT. This stance of US administration became visible during the Kargil war when it refused to buy any false arguments from Pakistan and instead put pressure on it to vacate the illegally occupied territory. The success achieved in the strategic dialogue culminated in President Clinton's visit to India in March 2000.

Constrained by NPT, India did not get official recognition of its nuclear weapon capability but issue of CTBT is not being pursued as US itself has not ratified CTBT.

Change in United States Perception

Over the past 15 years, three India specific developments have helped bring about the recent dramatic strengthening of U.S.-India ties. The events which had an overarching effect in this development were, first, the end of the Cold War removed the U.S.-Soviet rivalry as the principal focus of U.S. foreign relations and the rationale for India's nonalignment policy. Second, India's historic economic reforms of the early 1990s which opened India to

---

[9] http://www.un.org/News/Press/docs/1998/sc6528.doc.htm

the global economy for the first time and catalyzed the extraordinary boom in private-sector trade and investment between the United States and India that continues today. Finally, as the twenty-first century began, the global order started to undergo a tectonic shift and India's emergence as a global force.

Kargil Conflict 1999

In early 1999, Pakistan's regular and irregular forces crossed the LoC and occupied positions in the Kargil sector of Jammu and Kashmir, a foolhardy step to wrest Jammu and Kashmir in thick of insurgency sponsored by Pakistani ISI in the state of Jammu and Kashmir. When this was detected in early May 1999, Delhi's response was swift and comprehensive, involving the use of land and air forces to evict the intruders from the Indian side of the LoC. After several weeks of increasingly bloody conflict, Indian forces made substantiate progress and captured the key heights of Tololing (14 June) and Tiger Hill (early morning on 4 July). With Pakistani forces suffering critical defeats, it was only a matter of time before they were pushed back across the LoC. Feeling the pressure and looming setback in the Kargil War and concerned over Pakistan's increasing international isolation, Pakistani PM Nawaj Sharif went to United States to seek their intervention to stop the fighting and resolve the Kashmir issue. But contrary to their expectation, Bill Clinton came out heavy on Sharif and sought Pakistan withdrawal. The conflict in any case would have ended ultimately in favour of India but, the delay could have caused larger Indian casualties.

United States thus played a significant facilitation role in ending of the Kargil conflict which shortly afterwards saw the withdrawal of all Pakistani forces to its own side of the LoC without many additional Indian casualties. American facilitation on the Kargil conflict in Delhi's favour came as quite an unexpected surprise to many in India's Ministries of External Affairs and Defence. This was, in effect, the first time in fifty years that the United States had sided with India against Pakistan 'openly and firmly'.

It seems that the United States places a very high priority on improving relations between India and Pakistan and resolving the conflict over Kashmir — a potential nuclear flashpoint from their perspective.

Geo-Political & Economic Realities

The other factors that brought both countries closer are some developments with global ramifications. i.e. economic and military rise of China, war on terror, geopolitical situation in the Asia pacific region and Indian Ocean Region, global economic down turn, Chinese assertiveness and claim on the South China Sea which besides impinging on the freedom of innocent passage was against the established laws as laid down in the UN Convention on Laws of the Seas (UNCLOS).

Rise of China

Many around the world believe the global balance of power is shifting. The majority of the nations believe China eventually will replace the United States as the world's leading superpower. Of course, the U.S. is still the world's largest national economy almost three times large, yet a majority view that China would occupy a top position very soon is much more prevalent now. Energy is the key for the continued growth of China. China therefore, has become a key and very active player in the international geopolitics of energy. The Chinese energy trade with oil producing countries will bring with it a greater economic, political and military influence on these countries. Its territorial claims in the East China and South China seas is expression of this and has the potential of developing in to conflict with some of its neighbours. The expansion of the naval forces of the People's Liberation Army (PLA) is an expression of China's desire to protect the sea lanes it needs for transporting crude from the Middle East and West Africa. From the US perspective, China's energy policy creates several economic, environmental and geo-strategic challenges to Washington. To counter this it requires main players like India in the region. According to the former under secretary of state, Nicholas Burns," coping with a more powerful China will be the great challenge for the United States in the next half century, India may be the great opportunity——India is of immense strategic importance to the United States."[1]

However, many in India do not support any Indian role in any US-led containment of China. For India, keeping in view its socio economic strategic priority, an environment of peace is a pre-condition to pursue human development at an ever-increasing pace. Therefore in India's interests, they recommend cooperative relationship with China.

Economic Slow Down

Across the globe, the western economies had suffered the brunt of economic downturn more than the emerging economies say China, India and Brazil. Slowdown has not only affected their growth but brought in attendant problems like unemployment, implementing trade protective regimes like discouraging or dis-incentivising outsourcing of jobs outside. In this climate, U.S. and other Western economies look at India for closer trade relations particularly in arms trade in which India plans to spend over USD 80 billion in next five years. This means Industry's revival and jobs for the growing unemployed. India is seen as long-term investment opportunity. The United States has the technological edge to win Indian military contracts. In fact, in past the past three years, India agreed to buy more than $10 billion in U.S. military hardware. Even though the US firms lost the bid for an estimated USD 10 billion contract for sale of 126 jets to Indian Air Force (IAF), India is the third largest purchaser of US arms through the government to government channel, Foreign Military Sales (FMS) and hopes to corner biggest chunk from the expected $80 billion worth of India's arms purchase in the next five years. From India's side, the attraction is for better quality equipment than Russia our previous traditional arms supplier with fewer delays and re-negotiations such as happened with the carrier Admiral Gorshkov. From America's side, the attraction is a lucrative market in a secular, democratic, rising power.

---

[1] Economic Times, 3 Feb 2012, http://article.economictimes.indiatimes.com/2012-02-03/news/31021216 1nicholas-burns-india-trade-and-investment

War on Terror

Since the attacks of September 11, 2001, South Asia has been viewed in Washington as a region of vital importance. It is the region from which the United States was attacked by Al Qaeda. Pakistan and Afghanistan both have been identified as the harbinger and supporter of terror. India has been fighting the terror menace for more than two decades but, its fight was essentially its own fight which leave aside the support was not even acknowledged by Western nations including America. The U.S. fight against Al Qaeda brought in better appreciation of Indian predicament with Pakistan state sponsoring the terror. In fact, in the later part of the US campaign; American drones regularly target terrorists in Afghanistan and their hideouts in Federally Administered Tribal Areas (FATA) of Pakistan.

In the war against global terrorism, India was among the first few countries to offer assistance. In fact, during Operation Enduring Freedom in Afghanistan, the Indian Navy took up the important mission of escorting and protecting high value shipping through the Straits of Malacca.[2] This contribution freed US Naval ships to focus on other global commitments and, by allowing transiting US Naval ships to use Indian ports for rest and refuelling, India enabled logistical flexibility to US Navy to conduct its trans-oceanic operations. Allowing over-flight for US Air Force aircraft was another contribution by India that saved countless operational hours.

De-hyphenating of India and Pakistan

From the time of India's Independence till Clinton's visit in 2000, US policies toward South Asia was always considered a zero sum game with India and Pakistan having to be balanced against each other. Current Indo-U.S. relations are largely on their own merit and not linked to US Pakistan relations as before. Pakistan supports the U.S. war on terror in Afghanistan with facilitation of the supply line to Afghanistan in return of substantial economic package of USD 7.5 billon to be disbursed in five years.[3] It is quite akin to short term tactical cooperation between a country which is the principal victim of terrorism and a state which is its major perpetrator. India

---

[2] mod.nic.m/Samachar/sept15-02/html/ch6.htm

[3] Hindu ,25 Mar 2010

seems to be the natural partner for the United States in managing the Asian balance of power and a range of other global challenges as a rising power.

The Bush administration achieved the seemingly impossible: simultaneous improvement in U.S. relations with both India and Pakistan. While the public attention around the world was focused on Bush's historic civil nuclear initiative with India, his determined neutrality on the Kashmir question and his refusal to interpose the United States in this long-standing Indo-Pak dispute was critical in winning India's trust of the United States. Obama, however, initially signalled the prospect of a change in this policy by a renewed U.S. emphasis on Kashmir, which inevitably always led to the deepening of the Indo-U.S. divide. Obama's articulation hinted of the linkage between Afghanistan and Kashmir. His argument was simple: U.S. success in Afghanistan depends on fixing the problems in Pakistan. Those in turn depend upon ending Pakistan's insecurities vis-à-vis India, especially on Kashmir. Obama also seemed to believe that a comprehensive normalization of Indo-Pak relations will help stabilize and accelerate India's own rise as a great power. He sensed a rare diplomatic opportunity to forever transform Indo-Pak relations that would in turn serve U.S. interests in the region and pursued by appointing a special envoy to South Asia.

Obama persisted with a consistent articulation of the linkage between Afghanistan and Kashmir for long time till rebuffed by China which became more assertive economically and militarily which called for reappraisal of the south Asia policy and reverted to maintaining a neutral stand on Kashmir issue. Many however, still think that realistically for India to play a global role, geopolitical stability in its neighbour is pre –requisite.

Shift in U.S.-South Asia Policy.

U.S. sees India as a stabilizing force in an often violent and unstable part of the world. India offers a unique opportunity with real promise for the global balance of power. In the past decade, both President Bill Clinton and President George W. Bush recognized this opportunity and acted to construct a completely new foundation for U.S. ties with India. In January 2004, the United States and India agreed to expand cooperation in three specific areas: civilian nuclear activities, civilian space programmes, and high-technology trade. In addition, the two countries agreed to expand our dialogue on Missile

Defence. These areas of cooperation are designed to progress through a series of reciprocal steps that build on each other. The US befriending India to counter Chinese dominance has also ramifications in deterioration in US-Pakistan relations, especially since China and Pakistan have fostered a strong friendship for decades.

Asia Pacific Region

Asia-Pacific region is a "top priority" of US security policy. As part of a "rebalancing" in Asia-Pacific, the United States will enhance military-to-military cooperation with Asia Pacific states as well as boost the capabilities of its allies in the region, In pursuance of this, by 2020 the U.S. Navy will relocate its forces from present 50-50 split from the Pacific and Atlantic to a 60-40 split in these oceans. While United States has tried allaying fears of China which has criticised U.S stand, there is no doubt that it is meant to contain China's aggressive posture in the South China Sea. China has long-running territorial disputes with Southeast Asian countries over island groupings in the South China Sea and even claimed sovereignty on whole South China Sea. In recent years it has grown more assertive on the issue. The expansion of the Chinese Navy can be considered, at least in part, an expression of this aggressive Beijing's stance. This is already causing tension and could lead to disputes. United States believes that its military presence in the region will promote international order, peace and security in the region hence, it has decided to repostures its naval forces in the pacific as well as building and strengthening its alliances in Northeast/Southeast Asia and in the Indian Ocean Region. In this effort, United States has Identified India as a key partner. India while agreeing to the security concern of the Asia Pacific region and supports unhindered freedom of navigation in the international waters and stresses that contentious issues be settled in accordance with international laws.[4]

---

[4] The Hindu ,07 Jun 2012

Builiding of Defence Partenership

For building expanded cooperation and transforming their relationship India and United States signed number of agreements. In a journey towards building closer relationship, the Next Step in Strategic Partnership (NSSP) was the first such agreement which became a building block for further cooperation between them. President Bush shortly after the finalization of the agreement said, "In November 2001, Prime Minister Vajpayee and I committed our countries to a strategic partnership. Since then, our two countries have strengthened bilateral cooperation significantly in several areas. Today, we announce the next steps in implementing our shared vision."[1]

Next Steps in Strategic Partnership (NSSP). The United States and India announced in Jan 2004 major progress in the NSSP. Implementation of the NSSP was meant to lead towards significant economic benefits for both countries. This initiative gave a forward momentum to the mutual relationship towards a slow but steady expansion of military and strategic cooperation between the two countries.

By NSSP both countries agreed to expand cooperation in three specific areas: civilian nuclear activities, civilian space programs, and high-technology trade as well as to expand our dialogue on missile defence. These areas of cooperation are designed to progress through a series of reciprocal steps that build on each other. India was the only nuclear power outside of the formal system of US alliances that had been brought under an NSSP-style framework. It allowed the United States to engage India without openly accepting its status as a full-fledged nuclear power. Under phase 1 of NSSP,

---

[1] http://www.globalsecurity.org/military/world/india/nssp.htm

India and U.S. signed a High Technology Trade Agreement which implied "presumption of approval" for dual-use items that are not controlled for proliferation reasons. It also entailed removal of the headquarters of Indian Space Research Organisation (ISRO) from the Entity List.

Talks on Phase-II of the NSSP were held on October 21, 2004 when the US Assistant Secretary of State for South Asian Affairs, Christina Rocca, visited India. India reported "substantial progress" in four areas: biotechnology, nano technology, advanced information technology, and defence technology.[2]

New Framework in the India-US Defence Relationship 2005. This frame work was signed between the then Defence Minister, Pranab Mukerjee and US Defense Secretary, Donald Rumsfield on 28 Jun 2005, ten years after the "Agreed Minute" on defence relations between the United States and India was signed. The memorandum charted a future course for the broader strategic partnership between India and the United States. Under the New Framework, India and USA agreed to:

(a) Conduct joint and combined exercises and exchanges;

(b) Collaborate in multinational operations if it is in common interest;

(c) Strengthen capabilities of militaries to promote security and defeat terrorism;

(d) Promote regional and global peace and stability;

(e) Enhance capabilities to combat the proliferation of weapons of mass destruction;

(f) Increase opportunities for technology transfer, collaboration, co-production and research and development;

(g) Expand collaboration relating to missile defence;

(h) Strengthen abilities of the Armed Forces to respond quickly to disasters, including in combined operations;

---

[2] U.S.-India Next Steps in Strategic Partnership: Bureau of industry and security, U.S Depot of Commerce: http://www.bis.doc.gov/news/2004/us-indianextstep.htm

(i) Conduct successful peacekeeping operations;

(j) Conduct and increase exchanges of intelligence.

A large part of the understanding has been followed with usual complaints in some areas for their underperformance .For example there is a lot of ground is still to be covered in the sharing of the intelligence between the two nations.[3]

Concluded Defence Agreements. The Department of Defense of the United States of America and the Ministry of Defense of the Republic of India concluded several defence agreements to enhance cooperation and facilitate interaction.[4]

(a) **Agreement for Security Measures for Protection of Classified Military Information signed on January 2002 (GSOMIA).** On January 17, 2002, Defence Secretary Donald Rumsfeld and Defence Minister George Fernandes signed a US-India General Security of Military Information Agreement, in Washington "paving", in Rumsfeld's words, "the way for greater technology cooperation between the United States and India". Fernandes stated: "I am very happy that today...we have been able to revive our [military] relationship, and we look forward to much greater cooperation between the United States military and also procuring items that we need to procure from here.[5]

The GSOMIA essentially guaranteed that signing parties will protect any classified information/ technology shared between them. GSOMIA gave India access to greater military establishments and dual use technologies .It also paved the way for sale of U.S weapons to India. Almost immediately US government cleared licenses for twenty weapon systems for India.[6] In fact, just next

---

[3] merln.ndu.edu/merln/mipal/.../US_India_Defense_Framework.doc

[4] http://www.indianembassy.org/india-us-defense-relations.php

[5] Disarmament Diplomacy. Issue no: 63,Mar-Apr 63.http://www.acronym.org.uk/dd/dd63/63nr07.htm

[6] Page 90 of book US India cooperation in the 21st century: More than the words edited by sumit Ganguly and Andrew Scobell

day on signing of the agreement on February 18, General Richard Myers, the Chair of the US Joint Chiefs of Staff, announced that a deal to sell New Delhi a surveillance radar system was expected to be concluded soon.

(b) **Master Information Exchange Agreement (MIEA).** It was signed in February 2004 for standardization, rationalization, and interoperability of military equipment of both countries and to improve their mutual conventional defense capabilities through the application of emerging technologies and sharing of independently conducted research and development (R&D).[7]

(c) **Research Development Testing and Evaluation (RDT&E) Agreement** signed in January 2006. Recognising the benefits of the standardisation, rationalisation, and interoperability of military equipment, and seeking to make the best use of their respective research and technology as well as eliminate unnecessary duplication of work, encourage interoperability, efficient and cost effective research, development and evaluation projects are visualised with the object to improve the respective defence services conventional capabilities through the application of the emerging technologies.

(d) **Indo-U.S. Framework for Maritime Security Cooperation 2006.** In pursuance of this agreement India and the United States will address the non-traditional security threats, such as piracy, conventional and non-conventional arms proliferation and smuggling, environmental degradation and natural disasters [8]

How far these agreements have benefited India is not clear .In fact, Defence Minister; A K Anthony giving a reply to question on 15 Dec 2008 stated in Rajya Sabha that the Government has not made any study to assess the strategic benefits of India as well as USA out of these agreements.

---

[7] U.S.DoD and India MoD:Master Information Exchange Agreement:http://www.state.gov/documents/organization/161672.pdf

[8] http://www.defense.gov/news/Mar2006/d200600302indo usframe work formaritimesecuritycooperation.pdf

Indian Reservation on Some Agreements

India takes pride in maintaining an independent foreign policy and "strategic autonomy" therefore; it is not inclined to sign following agreements which in its view could compromise India's security and independence of security policy.

Proliferation Security Initiative (PSI). The PSI is a controversial U.S.-led multinational initiative involving the interdiction of third-country ships on the high seas. It was aimed to check transportation of nuclear proliferation material and equipment. The proposal has been criticised as apart from its doubtful legality, the PSI explicitly undercuts a genuinely multilateral and balanced approach to the problem of proliferation as it does not have approval of the United Nations. Among the major countries in Asia opposed to the PSI are China, Indonesia, Malaysia, and Iran.

Acquisition and Cross Servicing Agreement (re-named Logistics Support Agreement) it provides for use of each other's facilities and obtain refuelling and other services on credit during operations. The main concerns about LSA, is the need to designate ports and bases where the US would set up its logistical infrastructure, which is seen impinging our sovereignty by the critics.

The Communications Interoperability and Security Memorandum of Agreement (CISMOA). The agreement would facilitate air, sea and land assets of both sides can communicate with each other through common hardware and encryption software during as forces of US allies do during NATO operations. Critics of the agreement argue that with CISMOA in place U.S would establish backward linkages to the heart of the secure Indian Services 'communications systems and networks. Such linkages will permit the U.S. to penetrate and potentially disrupt and subvert the intra and inter Service communications setup and the military's communications with the Ministry of Defence and other agencies of the Government of India, involving extremely sensitive information, data, etc which is in conflict with the requirements of national security.⁹

The Basic Exchange and Cooperation Agreement (BECA). This facilitates exchange of geospatial information for the use of the Governments, defence and other government purposes.

The US argues that CISMOA and BECA will help the sale and transfer of advanced technologies and sensitive equipment to India. These will enhance interoperability of Indians with United States forces as equipments are usually installed in most US platforms. For instance, many of the on-board systems are not being cleared for sale by the U.S. government with the C-130J transport aircraft. The other requirement which India does not agree is to sign the End User agreement. Case specific CISMOA and End User agreement were signed with purchase of VVIP Business Boeing Jets but, the U.S. does not want to follow a case-by-case approach.[10]

It was asserted in Wikileaks an informal website that through these agreements, the U.S. intention was to bind India into a web of military relationships both for their immediate strategic dividends for the US Pacific Command embracing East and South East Asia, and as a part of the larger US strategy "to move the US-India mil-to-mil relationship closer. Another revelation by the wikileaks brought out that the US wanted to go even one step further and get India to agree to "Cooperative Security Locations" or CSLs, which are fully equipped military facilities in a dormant base that can be activated for operational use at short notice. This attracted criticism from even for pro-US sections of the Indian leadership.[11]

It was feared by the strategic community in India that the agreements would not only make India dependent but also compromise security. Air Chief Marshal PV Naik, the former Air Force Chief speaking at CII event on 15 Oct 10 ,has gone on record as saying that not signing of CISMOA would not affect his service's operational preparedness. There is general consensus that we cannot compromise the ability of our armed forces to be

---

[9] http://bharatkarnad.com/2011/11/18/india-america-the-future-of-a-strategic-partnership/

[10] Indian Express .29 nov 2009 http://www.indianexpress.com/news/for-key-defence-purchases-from-us-india-must-walk-obama-sweet-talk/546833/0

[11] http://newsclick.in/india/wikileaks-and-us-india-defence agreement

self-reliant especially in time of conflict when such equipment would actually be put to the use for which it was intended.[12] The Air Chief comments are based on sound commonsense as intrusive regimes have operational implications. But, inspite of our unwillingness to enter restrictive agreements, strategic partnership between the two countries is growing. U.S is merely complying domestic export controls and technology release policies to which US must conform under the Arms Export Control Act (AECA), which limits retransfer of munitions and imposes various measures which condition or accompany military sales or other defence transfers. U.S ships have in past used our ports as in the first Gulf War. Similarly, US aircraft had refuelled at the Indian airfields and U.S forces regularly exercise with the Indian forces. In recently unveiled 21st century security plan for Asia pacific, US while rebalancing its naval forces in Asia pacific is also seeking to develop closer partnership with India which entails unhindered transfer of high defence technology to India. U.S is no more pressing India to sign key pacts such as CISMOA and BECA that were earlier recognised as foundation agreements to strengthen Indo-US defence cooperation. US Defence Secretary during his visit of India on Jun 12 hinted that not signing these would not come in the way of taking military ties to higher level. He also confirmed that the US is working hard on export control reforms to improve their ability to transfer best technologies more quickly.[13] India should take advantage of this opportunity to develop indigenous defence industrial base.

---

[12] India Defence. http://www.india-defence.com/reports-4635

[13] India Today. http://indiatoday.intoday.in/story/leon-panetta-identifies-india-as-linchpin-to-counter-china/1/199505.html

Current Status of Partnership

Over the past decade, there has been a rapid transformation in the U.S.-India defence relationship. What was once a nascent relationship between unfamiliar nations has now evolved into a strategic partnership between two of the pre-eminent security powers in Asia. Today, U.S.-India defence ties are strong and growing. Our defence relationship involves a robust state of dialogues, military exercises, defence trade, personnel exchanges, and armaments cooperation. Our efforts over the past ten years have focused on relationship-building and establishing the foundation for a long-term partnership. There is a clear shift in American global and regional policy under which Washington now regards New Delhi as more an ally than just a partner. Confirming this Andrew Shapiro, Assistant Secretary of State for political-military affairs, said shortly after returning from India in April 2012 following a political- military dialogue between the two sides, the first such engagement in six years that, the regime of US high-technology denial to India is demonstrably over and India can now access a choice of US defence equipment available only to its closest partners. He also stressed that, " no two countries, not even allies, could be on the same page on all issues, but the commonality of US-India ties was so great that the partner-ally distinction was increasingly becoming a false one."[1] This though is an over statement, as like any close bilateral relations we also have different perception on several global issues yet in military interaction, we have experienced one of the closest defence relationship. In fact, India emerges as the third largest market for US Military Sales.

---

[1] Times of India, 28 April 2012

Formalised Structure for Mutual Interaction.

The defence cooperation has been institutionalised for its continuance and reliance. The 2005 New Framework Agreement provides the overarching structure for the U.S.-India defence relationship. The Defence Policy Group (DPG), chaired by the U.S. Under Secretary of Defence for Policy and the Indian Defence Secretary, is at the apex of the bilateral defence relationship. In addition to facilitating dialogue on issues of mutual interest, the DPG sets priorities for defence cooperation, reviews progress annually, and directs adjustments as necessary. Under the DPG umbrella, there are subgroups to discuss and advance defence trade, service-to-service cooperation, and technical cooperation, and technology security.[2] The recent 12th DPG meeting which concluded in New Delhi on 21st Feb. 2012 was co-chaired by U.S. Acting Under Secretary of Defence for Policy Dr. Jim Miller and Indian Defence Secretary, Shashikant Sharma. Later, Jim Miller gave his assessment in his statement to the Senate Armed Services Committee that, "a close, continuing, and expanding security relationship between the United States and India will be important for security and stability in Asia and for effectively managing Indian Ocean security in the 21st century."[3] Various institutional mechanisms under the DPG which coordinate and implement defence cooperation in specific areas include:

(a) **Defence Joint Working Group (DJWG)** – This undertakes mid-year review of progress made in the fulfilment of decisions taken by the DPG. It also reviews matters, which need to be taken up by the DPG.

(b) **Senior Technology Security Group (STSG)** – This is charged with undertaking review of technology security issues and also increase mutual understanding of each other's policies and systems in respect of technology security for defence-related equipment.

---

[2] http://www.defense.gov/pubs/pdfs20111101_NDAA_ Report_on_US_ India_Security_ Cooperation.pdf

[3] PTI 30Mar 2012. http://www.newsbullet.in/world/52-more/27969-defence-ties-with-india-strong-pentagon

(c) **Defence Procurement and Production Group (DPPG)** – this reviews opportunities for cooperation in defence acquisition, transfer of technology/collaboration and defence related industries.

(d) **Joint Technical Group (JTG)** – this look at potential for cooperation in defence research and development.

(e) **Military Cooperation Group (MCG)** – reviews Services-related cooperation matters and inter-service coordination.

(f) **Service-to-Service Executive Steering Groups (ESGs)** – these review service-to-service cooperation and report to the Military Cooperation Group.[4]

Initiation of Strategic Dialogue

Since Jun 2009, U.S. Secretary of State Ms. Hillary Clinton and Indian Foreign Minister SM Krishna established annual bilateral Strategic Dialogue. The first dialogue was held at Washington, the second at New Delhi in 2011 and third dialogue once again was held in Jun 2012 at Washington. The consultations cover the entire gamut of global and regional issues; economic, trade and investment; clean energy and climate change; education and development; and science and technology, health, innovation and not military alone. Such interactions have created better understanding of each other and a positive environment for closer cooperation in all areas including the defence.

Defence Relationship

Beginning in 1995, over the past decade, there has been a rapid transformation in the U.S.-India defence relationship.

Operational Co-operation. The United States and India have partnered closely on humanitarian assistance and disaster relief. In 2005, we introduced the U.S.-India Disaster Response Initiative (DSI) to spur greater training and engagement and to prepare for combined responses to future disasters in the Indian Ocean Region. Additionally, the U.S. Navy and Indian Navy have cooperated operationally on four separate occasions:

---

[4] http://www.indianembassy.org/india-us-defense-relations.php

security by the Indian Navy for U.S. ships transiting the Strait of Malacca after 9/11; disaster relief efforts after the Indian Ocean Tsunami in 2004-2005; non combatant evacuation operations in Lebanon in 2006; and counter-piracy operations in the Gulf of Aden since 2008[5].

Joint Training Exercises. The Kicklighter proposals in nineties following Gen Rodrigues interaction enabled the first ever Indo-US military-to-military level exercises. Consequently, in February 1992, Indian and US Army and Air Force paratroopers held their first joint training exercise codenamed "Teak Iroquois". A similar exercise, "Balance Iroquois", was held between Indian Para Commandos and US Special Forces in June 1995 near Paonta Sahib in India. The second round was conducted in Madhya Pradesh in March/April1997.The Marine Special Forces also conducted joint exercises, named "Flash Iroquois", in September 1994 and September 1996.[6]

U.S.-India Military Exercises have improved in scale and frequency since the signing of the New Framework in 2005. We now have regular exercises across all services that help to deepen our military and defence relationships. Indian Army has been involved in joint exercises (Ex-Shatrujeet since 2006, Indo-U.S. mechanised ex Yudh Abhyas since 2004, Counter Insurgency and Jungle Warfare Ex Vajra Prahar since 2003 etc) with the US Army on low intensity conflict in jungle terrain, counter terrorism and counter insurgency are regularly held at India / United states. The exercises have tremendous benefits for both India and U.S as Indian forces gain from the experience of interacting with force with better technological hardware whereas , India's diverse terrain is Ideal to train under any conditions .In addition , they also get the advantage of learning from the vast Indian experience in Anti-guerrilla warfare and in fighting insurgency. In fact, subsequent to 2005 USCENTCOM sought to exercise in the Siachin which however, was not accepted by India.

---

[5] Report to US congress on US-India Security Co-operation by US Depot of Defence Nov2011;http://www.defense.gov/pubs/pdfs/20111101_ NDAA_Report_on_ US_India_Security Cooperation.pdf

[6] An Article titled,' Indo-US Defense and Military Relations : From Estrangement to Strategic Partnership. By VP Malik in US-Indian Strategic Co-operation in to the 21st century- More than words. Edited by Sumit Ganguly,Brian Shoup and Andrew Scobell

Naval cooperation between the United States and India helped to lay the groundwork for military-to-military cooperation and our exercises continue to evolve in complexity. Both navies conduct four exercises annually: MALABAR, HABU NAG (naval aspects of amphibious operations), SPITTING COBRA (explosive ordnance destruction focus), and SALVEX (diving and salvage). [7]

Malabar is a premier annual exercise with the US and other navies of the region viz; Japan Australia and Singapore to reinforce maritime tactics, techniques, and procedures (TTPs) of nations and involves contraband control operations, sea control operations, air defence exercises, sea replenishment including fuel transfer, cross-deck flying etc. The exercises have been regularly held since 1992 with a brief interlude after the India's nuclear test in 1998 and were resumed again from 2002 onwards following Sep11 terror attack at New York. In the recent Malabar exercise from 09 Apr – 16 Apr 2012, both ashore and at-sea training was conducted. While ashore in Chennai, India, training included subject matter expert and professional exchanges on counter-piracy operations, carrier aviation operations, maritime patrol and reconnaissance operations and anti-submarine warfare operations. The at-sea portions was conducted in two phases. Phase I took place in the vicinity of Chennai, while Phase II in the Bay of Bengal and west of the Nicobar Islands. The exercises are designed to advance participating nations' military-to-military coordination and capacity to plan and execute tactical operations in a multinational environment.[8] Indian Navy finds considerable value in the experience gained from joint exercises using modern networking systems, and also looks positively at the prospect of strengthening deep-water capabilities through such joint collaborations. The U.S. Coast Guard, with the support of the Departments of Defence and Homeland Security, has also recently begun engagement and training with the Indian Coast Guard.[9]

---

[7] Report to US congress on US-India Security Co-operation by US Depot of Defence Nov2011;http://www.defense.gov/pubs/pdfs/20111101_NDAA_Report_on_US_India_Security_Cooperation.pdf

[8] http://indiandefenceboard.com/threads/indo-usa-malabar-exercise-2012.1874/

[9] Report to US congress on US-India Security Co-operation by US Depot of Defence Nov2011;http://www.defense.gov/pubs/pdfs 0111101_NDAA_Report_on_US_India_Security_Cooperation.pdf

Current Status of Partnership

In 2011, a total of 56 cooperative events across all Services were held with United Sates, more than India conducted with any other country. In 2010, the U.S. Pacific Command (USPACOM) and the Indian Integrated Defence Staff (IDS) conducted the inaugural Joint Exercise India (JEI) tabletop exercise in Alaska. JEI is a joint, combined exercise based on a Humantarian Assistance/ Disaster Relief (HA/DR) scenario and is a significant step in the evolution of our exercise programme because it facilitates multi service and bilateral cooperation.[10]

The Indian Air Force and U.S AF have participated in Joint air exercises EX RED FLAG, at the Nellis AFB, USA in August 2008. RED FLAG is a joint, combined training exercise that provides a peacetime "battlefield" to train interoperability across a variety of mission sets, including interdiction, air superiority, defence suppression, airlift, aerial refuelling, and reconnaissance. The IAF intends to participate in Ex. RED FLAG, Nellis in 2013 as well with both fighters and airborne warning and control system aircraft.

In Cope India 2004 at Gwalior and in 2005 and 2006 at Kalaikunda base, IAF played host to United States Air Force F15, F-16s and an E3C Sentry AWACS[11] [12] and at Agra 2009 in an airlift exercise that provides training for humanitarian assistance and disaster relief operations. A combined total of 25 sorties were flown on the C-17 Globe master III and C-130 H and J Hercules during the exercise, which took place at different locations and had great learning value for both the Air Forces.[13] In June 2010, the U.S. Air Force (USAF) and IAF conducted a UNIFIED ENGAGEMENT seminar focused on planning for future employment of airpower concepts, including: intelligence, surveillance, and reconnaissance planning; targeting hardened and deeply-buried targets; and combat search and rescue operations[14]

---

[10] Ibid

[11] News Report by Jayant Gupta ,20 Nov 2005, Times of India

[12] http://www.bharat-rakshak.com/IAF/Images/Special/Exercises CopeIndia2006US/

[13] A Report by Capt. Genieve David of 13th Air Force Public Affairsin official Website of US Air Force http://www.af.mil/news/story.asp?id=123174977

[14] Ibid

Counterterrorism: The 2010 Counterterrorism Cooperation Initiative opened the door for increased cooperation and collaboration on counterterrorism (CT) issues. We will continue to seek greater cooperation in information-sharing activities as well as in our training, exercises, and exchanges between CT specialists and on CT capabilities. USPACOM seeks to increase its Joint Combined Exchange Training exercises with India. Additionally, it will continue to train higher-ranking officers through the Combating Terrorism Fellowship Program (CTFP), which, in FY11, succeeded in training two dozen Indian officers attended during various CT related courses and seminars conducted by U.S.[15]

Defence Sales. The increasing convergence between Indian and US defence establishments is manifested in the signing of several major procurement contracts between the two countries. Several US companies are competing to supply defence equipment to India as part of the Indian armed forces ongoing modernization programme. Starting at zero, the Foreign Military Sales (FMS) from United States have grown to a combined total value of approximately $8 billion. With India planning to buy in excess of $100 billion worth of new weapons over the next ten years, arms sales can provide impetus to India- U.S. defence relations.

Since 2002, India has signed more than 20 Foreign Military Sales (FMS) comprising high value sale of defence articles and services such as ten heavy airlift **Boeing C-17** valued $5.8 billion for the strategic roles with an option to purchase six more The delivery will take place in 2013and 2014. The C-17's advantages include its easier handling (compared with the IL-76) and ability to operate from short and rough airstrips .Its induction would augment Indian military's ability to quickly lift larger numbers of troops wherever needed to quickly strengthen its presence.

Six C-130J aircraft for the Special Forces has been procured form U.S Lockheed Martin Company for $964 million, another six has been contracted. C-130J's will significantly enhance capability with the aircraft ability to land and take off even in improvised or short airfields, and without

---

[15] A Report by Capt. Genieve David of 13th Air Force Public Affairsin official Website of US Air Force http://www.af.mil/news/story.asp?id=123174977

lights. India's interest in the Hercules is quite specific to the Special Forces at the moment; but the plane's capacity for additional specialty operations like aerial refuelling enhances those operations, and gives the IAF a number of additional employment options and have already been successfully employed to provide critical humanitarian assistance following an earthquake in Sikkim in September 2011.

P-8i Neptune. Indian naval responsibilities are growing, and especially after the 2008 Mumbai attack the surveillance and control of sea coast has become a necessity. It urgently needed to replace Soviet TU142. India has signed a deal of $2.1 billion with U. S. for eight Boeing P8i jets in January 2009. India's Navy may extend the buy, and enlarge its fleet of Boeing P-8 Poseidon aircraft to 12. The naval top brass feels that by 2020 India could be looking for 30 aircraft.[16] The confirmed onboard weapons at this time include the Mk-54 lightweight torpedo, which can be enhanced with the HAAWC kit for high-altitude,[17] GPS-guided drops. For longer-range surface attacks, AGM-84 Harpoon Block II missiles are carried on external pylons. A number of electronic and sensor systems will differ due to Indian insistence on indigenous content and American security concerns that forced the use of alternatives.

The Indian Navy currently relies on its fleet of around 15 Dornier 228-101 aircraft and 12 Israeli Searcher Mark II and Heron unmanned aerial vehicles to monitor India's 7,516 km long coastline, 1,197 islands and a 2.01 square km exclusive economic zone. Additional patrols and interdiction within and beyond that area are undertaken by its 8 ultra-long-range TU-142 Bear aircraft and its IL-38 maritime surveillance aircraft, which have been upgraded to IL-38SD status. Boeing's P-8i's fast long-range cruise, and advanced ground and ocean monitoring systems are the best option for patrolling the Indian Ocean's vast expanses. Procurement of modern

---

[16] http://www.defenseindustrydaily.com/indias-navy-holding-maritime-patrol-aircraft-competition-updated-01991/

[17] The High Altitude ASW Weapons Concept (HAAWC).This LongShot system is a low-cost, self-contained wing adaptor kit that can provide long distance precision capabilities to a range of existing air-to-surface munitions, including sea mines, gravity bombs, laser-guided bombs and cluster bomb dispensers. The system is self-contained and includes a flight control computer, a GPS-based navigation system, and power sources; range is up to 50 nautical miles.It is a potential competitor to Boeing's Joint direct attack munition (JDAM).

maritime patrol aircraft would certainly expand India's capabilities, as its naval responsibilities undergo rapid growth. To the west, India is also undertaking anti-piracy efforts on the East African coast, with a base in Madagascar and a recent military cooperation agreement with Mozambique includes coastal patrol responsibilities.[18]

Ultra Light Howitzers. The contract for supply of 145 ultra light howitzers by BAe Systems valued at USD 647 million has been concluded. The deal had been facing the legal hurdles, and is being procured through foreign military sale route with direct government-to-government contract between the US and the Indian governments.[19]

Harpoon Block II Anti-ship Missiles. 24 Harpoon Block-II anti-ship missiles, worth USD 170 million, to arm the maritime strike Jaguar fighters in IAF's combat fleet. The Harpoon Block II is the latest version of the subsonic missile and is able to strike land-based targets and ships. It is an all-weather, over the horizon, anti-ship missile which can be launched from surface ships, submarines and aircraft.

The other sales include TPQ-37 Fire finder Radars, Self-protection Suites (SPS) for VVIP aircraft, for IAF and The former USS TRENTON, which was transferred to the Indian Navy in 2007 and christened the INS JALASHWA, has helped the Indian Navy expand its amphibious and expeditionary warfare capabilities. As can be seen that, India has not purchased routine defence equipment but, which primarily has enhanced the strategic and expeditionary capability of the defence forces.[20] The 12th Defence plan too focuses on building navy's expeditionary capability. Similar to earlier acquired Landing Platform Dock (LPD) INS Jal Ashwa, India will float tender for additional four LPD's to upgrade its amphibious capabilities. The objective to build adequate standoff capability for sealift

---

[18] Defence Industry daily.P8i : Indian navy picks its future high end Maritime Patrol aircraft.http://www.defenseindustrydaily.com/indias-navy-holding-maritime-patrol-aircraft-competition-updated-01991/

[19] Media report

[20] Report to US congress on US-India Security Co-operation by US Depot of Defence Nov2011;http://www.defense.gov/pubs/pdfs 20111101_NDAA_Report_ on_ US_India_Security_Cooperation.pdf

and expeditionary operations to achieve desired power projection force levels, influence events on the shore and undertake military operations other than war.[21]

India's is also making effort to build its domestic defence industry hence, agreements focus with transfer of technology. India's own LCA whose deliveries to IAF are slated to commence from 2014 has initially sourced its engines F104 and F414 from General Electric, an American company to power its MKI and MKII aircraft till it develops its own engine. A total of 49 GE F404 and 99 GE F414 engines have been contracted with transfer in technology for in-house development of the engines.[22] In its quest towards modernisation India may procure geavy lift and combat helicopters, anti tank missiles, engines for Jaguar aircraft, quick reaction surface to Air missiles in time to come which American companies may successfully bid and get contracts.

Personnel Exchanges. There is a fair level interaction between U.S. and Indian defence personnel. To take one example, the U.S. and Indian Air Forces currently maintain a standing T-38/Kiran instructor pilot exchange between Columbus Air Force Base, Mississippi and AFS Hakimpet in Hyderabad, India. Many other personnel exchange opportunities exist which enhances familiarity with each country's armed forces, strengthens professionalism, and facilitates cooperation during bilateral exercises and strategy discussions. Courses included Army War College, Air Command and Staff College, Naval Staff College, International Officer Preparation, the Judge Advocate Staff Officer Course, and training in medical services, aircraft maintenance and maritime search/rescue. Additionally, the Asia Pacific Centre for Security Studies (APCSS) has hosted more than 200 military and civilian Indian participants across all ministries[23] including the scholars of prominent Indian Think Tanks (IDSA and CENJOWS) in their multilateral Southeast Asian security awareness programmes.

India in U.S. Security Policy Statements

Prior to the year 1998, India hardly found any mention in U.S. security

---

[21] Indian Express. 4th May 2012.
[22] Business Standard of 01 Oct 2010
[23] Ibid

policy statements except for negative reasons such as high population density, pollution and degradation in environment and to stress U.S. nuclear and missile proliferation concerns with ultimate aim to cap, reduce and, ultimately, eliminate the nuclear and missile capabilities of India and Pakistan. In 1998 for the first time, United States inequitably stated that it "seeks to establish relationships with India and Pakistan that are defined in terms of their own individual merits and reflect the full weight and range of U.S. strategic, political and economic Interests in each country."[24]

From United States perspective, India is seen as a partner to reassert U.S. hegemony in Asia where now it faces competition from growing economic and military power of China. The U.S. security policy statements after year 1999 seem to indicate this security concern.

President Clinton visit of India in March 2000 followed with PM Vajpayee visit of America six months later in Sep 2000 gave a clear signal of India U.S. rapprochement. **The US National Security Strategy, 2000** indicated the path for future Indo-US Co-operation. The document stated, "After the President's visit to India, we are working to enhance our relationship with India at all levels. We look forward to more frequent high level contacts including meetings between our heads of government and our cabinet officials."[25]

Major push to Indo-US relations was given by President Bush who on taking over his office in 2001, recognized the importance of India's large and vibrant democracy in global politics .U.S strategic community acknowledges that with growing economy ,military capability and stable democratic institutions, India is poised to matter significantly in the Asian balance of power. If Washington is to promote liberal democracy in Asia it can not ignore India which has the potential to become one of the democratic powers of twenty-first century. In **Security Strategy of 2002**, U.S ranks India in the category of "potential great powers".[26] As result of this assessment, United States has sought to engage India. This marked the

---

[24] National Security Strategy for a New Century. White House, Oct 1998. http://www.au.af.mil/au/awc/awcgate/nss/nssr-1098.pdf

[25] http://www.bits.de/NRANEU/others/strategy/nss-0012.pdf

[26] http://merln.ndu.edu/whitepapers/USnss2002.pdf

beginning of U.S. India engagement in security and Defence matters.

United States has once again stressed about India and United States partnership in the United States **National Security Strategy of 2010** it calls both nations to work together through mutual Strategic Dialogues and high-level visits and sought a broad-based relationship with India towards global counterterrorism and non-proliferation effort among other issues such as poverty-reduction, education, health, and sustainable agriculture. Bush expressed confidence in India's growing leadership on a wide array of global issues, through groups such as the G-20, and sought to work with India to promote stability in South Asia and elsewhere in the world.[27]

President Obama too has asserted about investing in long term U.S. India security partnership to tackle challenges in Asia /Asia-pacific and in the Indian Ocean region and in fighting global war on terror in the **New Strategic Guidance** issued to Department of Defence (DoD) on 05 Jan 2012 .[28]

Industry Linkages

The progressive policy level changes initiated by the government of India coupled with normalisation of India's geopolitical relationships have provided a significant opportunity to Indian Industry to enter the defence manufacturing sector. It can take advantage of the offset clause of Defence Procurement Policy (DPP) which specifies that a foreign armament company which bags an arms deal over Rs.300 crores must plough back at least 30% of the contract value back in to India as an offset and through participation in maintenance and overall opportunity. In $20billion MMRCA deal actually specifies a must 50% offset on the foreign vendor[29]. With growing business, Airbus and Boeing are understood to be considering setting up Maintenance and Repair Organisation (MRO) facilities in India. Additionally, the US Defence firm Raytheon has signed an agreement with India's Elcom Marine Company to provide spare support for the maintenance of Phalanx close-in weapon system on board Indian Navy's INS Jalashwa amphibious warship.

---

[27] http://www.whitehouse.gov/sites/default/files/rss_viewer national_security_strategy.pdf
[28] http://www.defense.gov/news/Defense_Strategic_Guidance.pdf
[29] Times of India, New Delhi. 15 May 12

Euro copter, has also announced that it would establish an MRO facility to serve the large Dauphin fleet being operated in India. The Tata Group, for example, has already signed agreements with several international companies, including one to manufacture components for Boeing. Tata have established a new company, Nova Integrated Systems Limited to develop manufacture and support a wide range of defence and aerospace products. Such measures will allow the group to fulfil its vision of moving into full-scale aircraft assembly and production in both the civil and military markets. Similarly, the British Aerospace tie-up with the Mahindra Group primarily is with the twin objectives of broadening their market access to supply components to the Original Equipment Manufacturers (OEM) and global defence primes directly and also allowing them to adequately leverage their manufacturing capabilities domestically. The AEROINDIA and annual DEFEXPO shows have seen very good participation from US companies in recent times, an indicator of their serious interest in the Indian defence market. Several major US defence corporations have established presence in India and are operating directly (Boeing, Lockheed Martin, GE, to name a few). Indian Industry is set to gain in capacity with sizeable funds are earmarked for modernisation of Armed forces (approx 100 billion in next ten years). The offset have already zoomed to $4 billion as on May 12 was stated by the Defence Minister in the parliament and is indicative of the future gain of the Indian Industry.[30]

Tsunami Disaster Management

On December 26, 2004, in the wake of the tsunami disaster and the subsequent humanitarian catastrophe, India and the United States geared up for an unprecedented military cooperation in the Indian Ocean. The strategic implications of disaster management efforts in the tsunami-affected areas were:

(a) India's refusal of aid from abroad reflected its self-confidence and power. Its swift action showed that India was a strong, independent global player. Its offers of help improved it's standing with neighbours, and also re- established its image as a regional leader.

---

[30] Ibid

(b) It served to reaffirm India's "Look East" policy and strengthen its ties with Southeast Asia.

(c) For the first time, Indian and US forces coordinated humanitarian work in the Indian Ocean region. Growing military-to-military contacts between the two countries over the past several years—a centrepiece of new Indo-US relationship—made it possible for the two states to play a leading and coordinated role in relief. Indo-US cooperation during the period also showed that latent suspicions of American initiatives in the region that until recently preoccupied India's foreign Policy is declining rapidly. About 40,000 military personnel from more than a dozen nations participated in aid operations around the Indian Ocean. Close working relationships among the armed forces of a number of countries during relief work opened further possibilities of cooperative security in the region.

Bottlenecks in Defence Cooperation

Defence and military relations are always sensitive to political and strategic shifts. Although the Clinton- Vajpayee took bold steps in changing the nature and scope of Indo-US relations, particularly by moving away from the traditional non-proliferation prism to include economic, political, and strategic interests, it was the Bush-Man Mohan Singh that made it a reality. The Bush administration, in addition to putting some pressure on Pakistan to stop terrorism across the LoC, took positive steps in removing sanctions and renewed military ties with India. Despite limited arms and technology transfers from the United States, it is important to note that transfers did not take place easily with India, in sharp contrast to the United States experience with Pakistan. A 2003 Pentagon Report, "Indo-US Military Relationship: Expectations and Perceptions," highlights some bottlenecks in furthering defence relationship:-

(a) There is persistent internal bureaucratic wrangling in United States and India between various departments resulting in avoidable delays. United States. Department of defence officials often maintain that the State Department still has a Cold War framework in its policies toward South Asia. State Department officials often argued that any arms transfer to India, in particular Missile Defence Systems, would adversely impact the military balance of the region, in addition to a possible breach of the 1987 Missile Technology Control Regime (MTCR).

(b) The critics of US India defence cooperation also complain that the United States is not a reliable partner on account of its strategic ties with Pakistan and thus would not prefer the weapon system which is held by Pakistan moreover, it avoided giving long-term strategic commitments or assurances to India. Further, there is fear of future sanctions; Former US Ambassador Robert Blackwill admitted that the US could not ensure an "uninterrupted supply of spare parts and customer support for defence equipment over 30 years, as that would necessitate constitutional changes." Similar concern has been expressed by then Defence Minister Shri Pranab Mukherjee in the Aero-India 2005 that India is keen on US equipment and on "diversifying" its equipment suppliers, but US laws leave buyers of American equipment sanctions-prone. India is to be reasonably assured its defence equipment won't be affected by "sanctions."[31]

(c) Indo-US defence relations also remain affected by the following dynamics:

  (i) Different Perceptions of the World Order. India recognizes US pre-eminence in the global strategic architecture but also recognizes the pressing need for developing a cooperative multi-polar world order.

  (ii) Fears of US Indifference to Pakistan related security Concerns of India. There is a continuing apprehension in India about the persistent issue of Indo-Pak hyphenation even though the recent official US responses to regional events signal otherwise.

  (iii) The United States Nuclear Non-proliferation Objectives. There is considerable scope for convergence and mutual co-operation in this field provided the United States accepts the reality of

---

[31] US- India Strategic cooperation in to the 21st century : More than the words By Sumit Ganguly nad Andrew Scobell ,page 95

India as a nuclear nation.

(iv) India's reservations on buying weapons, defence equipment and technology from the United States due the fears of future sanctions and lack of assurance of uninterrupted supply of spare parts and customer support.

(v) Continuing Misperceptions and Lack of Confidence in the Mind of Bureaucrats in the United States and Political Leaders in India.

(vi) India's Pride in Maintaining an independent foreign policy and "Strategic Autonomy" also seems likely to set limits on bilateral security cooperation. India continues to spearhead opposition to US positions in multilateral forums, particularly on environmental and on trade issues. Moreover, New Delhi has systematically kept its options open with diverse nations— Russia, the European Union countries, Central Asian states, Iran, Israel, and Persian Gulf Arab nations, for example— reflecting its sense of a unique destiny and prickliness about US pressure, as well as a desire to ensure energy and military supplies and to checkmate China's and Pakistan's foreign relations.

(vii) Washington's and New Delhi's China policies differ as well. India still suffers from some "China envy" but will continue to sidestep US suggestions that it serve as a counterweight to China. India was part of Informal security dialogue initiated by Japan between U.S, Australia, and Japan in 2007. The arrangement is widely viewed as a response to increased Chinese economic and military power but, India has refuted any such any anti China alliance. In the words of PM Man Mohan Singh," I have made it clear to the Chinese leadership that India is not part of any so-called contain China effort," he told reporters when asked about the four-nation security dialogue among the U.S., Japan, Australia and India. The dialogue remains disrupted due the Australian as well as Indian reluctance to join arrangement which can be construed as an alliance.[32] But, India is strengthening relations with Japan and Southeast Asia as an insurance against Beijing's "encirclement strategy."

(viii) Agreements such as the End-Use Agreements which the US normally insists on for government-to-government sales, and which gives the US rights to inspect military equipment sold to other countries on site and determine how they are used. Similar opposition is to BECA and CISMOA which U.S insists are essential for sale of high technology and sensitive equipment. Anti U.S lobby asserts that the US; military sales to India are essentially seen not as ends in themselves but as part of a larger goal of drawing India into the US geo-strategic orbit. This may not be entirely correct as defence sales though crucial are not the sole component of a broader geo-strategic alliance. However, it seems that after unveiling of security plan for Asia Pacific US may not insist on signing of these restrictive /intrusive agreements as prerequisite for transfer high defence technology to India even though sales are through FMS route. U.S. defence Secretary, Leon Panetta even assured that US administration would work hard to soften US Congress stand for transfer of sophisticated defence technology to India which as per their law is restricted.

(ix) Reluctance by US to link sale with the transfer of technology which is necessary to boost the domestic defence Industry. India does not fully trust the U.S. after its experience with the nuclear explosions in the 90s, when the U.S. put sanctions on India. What if it was to do that again, especially in the middle of a war? U.S. transactions are still constrained by nuclear dual-use concerns. However, recent wikileaks disclosures show that US officials both in the US and especially in the Embassy in New Delhi are aware of strong Indian requirement for technology transfer to accompany any military sales. Cables reveal the US establishment though not being accustomed to

---

[32] Hindu 11 Jan 2008. http://www.hindu.com/2008/01/11/stories/2008011164001200.htm

such arrangements is gradually coming around to the idea in the interest of promoting the strategic partnership it wants "at a time when the goal of establishing a key strategic relationship... with one of Asia's rising giants... is becoming reality." India has carried out purchase of defence equipment mainly due our transparency concerns. FMS sales besides denying the contractual leverage which is normally available in competition also leads restrictive sale regime which as per US law, permits transfer of sophisticated technology on meeting conditions. Moreover, weapon purchase through FMS route adds costs and suffers from lethargic processing in the US bureaucracy. The US officials suggest that the Defence Production and Procurement Group set up under the Defence Agreement could lay the foundation for direct interaction among Indian and U.S. business leaders aimed at creating corporate structures as the basis for defence cooperation, beginning with a few discreet projects.[33]

A workable strategy can be evolved by the business leaders to initiate the near absent domestic defence Industry. The government has not only liberalized the offsets regime by various means including opening up civilian sector offsets which would benefit companies such as Boeing but has also decisively opened up the defence sector to the private sector including with foreign collaboration which will promote both U.S and Indian Interests.

---

[33]http://newsclick.in/india/wikileaks-and-us-india-defence-agreement

Challenges Ahead

Indian Internal Politics. After the US and the coalition forces, in 2003, attacked and captured Iraq, there were expectations in US circles that India would contribute to coalition forces in Iraq. When India declined to send troops to Iraq, due to lack of political consensus within the country and for other reasons, there was considerable disappointment in the United States. Nevertheless, the disjuncture demonstrated that India's domestic political constraints might produce outcomes that run counter to US expectations. Without adequate understanding of such political factors in the two nations, there will always be a danger of a derailment of defence ties.

The present coalition government in Delhi is heavily dependent on support from alliance partners. This affects mutual relations which also impinge on defence cooperation realm.

New Geo-Strategic Realities. While major differences over foreign policy between India and the United States have gone. We still have to come to terms with certain ground realties. Developing close relations with US are not at the cost of strategic imperatives which India will have to consider. Most important is Iran. While the United States would prefer India not to have any connection with Teheran, for New Delhi, Iran it is not only a close neighbour but also a major source of its energy requirements. Iran is also important for India's West Asia policy and an entry point to Central Asia and for meeting India's energy need which can hardly be replaced in entirety .

India–China–US Trilateral Relationships. A balance will have to be maintained in the trilateral relations so that the positions are not misread which can become source of tension. India need to take advantage of Indo-U.S closeness but for this it will have to maintain a fine balance in cooperative multilateral arrangements like SCO, RIC etc which can be misread by United

Challenges Ahead

States. India needs to allay U.S. suspicion about this being an anti U.S. lobby. India should not participate in pronouncements which patently are anti U.S. for it is likely that China and Russia could use these forums to progress their agenda. Their pronouncements on Ballistic Missile Defence and in the realm of Space Security are the cases on this point.

Pakistan. Today the United States treats Pakistan and India as separate actors important to it for different reasons. But still India at times continues to articulate deep concerns whenever US arms sale to Pakistan is carried out . We should get out of this mind set Indo US relations are not zero sum game vis-à-vis its relations with Pakistan. In the past, this perception in India has harmed India's interest. It appears that there is a vested interest among all parties that India- Pakistan now to improve relations. This has coincided with Pakistan military loosing some clout. Will this continue and be sustained leading to genuine and substantive cooperation? If it were to be so a major irritant in Indo-US relations will be set aside.

Lack of an Arms Supply Relationship. Realistically, a true strategic relationship cannot develop in a state of limited arms and technology trade. India's must have reasonable expectations of reliability of supply, availability of the latest weaponry packages, technology transfer, reasonable cost and permission to manufacture in country.

Support to the US on the Global War on Terrorism. A true strategic partnership also calls for substantive mutual cooperation by India and U.S. on fight against terror.Support from U.S. is still perfunctory. Anti terror action by U.S. against terror groups that attack US interests and not the others leads to trust deficit.

A Way Ahead

Make Progress on nuclear trade. The implementation of the U.S.-India Civil Nuclear Agreement and engaging in significant civil nuclear trade would create positive momentum in the bilateral strategic relationship and help to facilitate U.S. Defence trade with India. A beginning has been made with recent signing of contrcat by GE to establish two nuclear power plant of 1000MW each in Gujarat.

Revise Indian Defence Procurement Policy. To develop indigenous industry it is essential to make offsets succeed. A most important way is to increase the FDI limit beyond 26 per cent so that the US and other foreign firms will have more incentives to invest in new Indian ventures and so that they will have enough authority over those ventures for confidence in the quality and timeliness of product. This is especially needed if the offset programme is to succeed in bringing aerospace and defence work to companies outside the 'top tier' of India's private sector industrial enterprises.

Co-Developing Technology. We need to persuade United States for deeper defence industrial cooperation with India, including a range of cooperative research and development activities. In fact, after rejection of US contenders in the MMRCA the sources in the United States had offered even top end ac F-35 with India. As India is already jointly developing FGFA with Russia; hence, this offer has not been accepted. United States remains a contender in arms purchase, but not first choice because of the conditions attached with the sales such as transfer of technology, end use of the equipment. In view of this, India presently is buying its immediate needs such as fighter jets, from both Europeans and Russians, who are less likely than the United States to attach conditions to such purchases. However, it will continue to buy from the United States items unrelated to immediate threats, such as power-projection equipment, though New Delhi has no immediate plans to conduct expeditionary warfare. Dr. Stephen P. Cohen in an interview to National Bureau of Asian Research has argued that to overcome India's worry on supply reality the United States should co-develop technology with India, as it does with Israel. Since new technology is not yet developed, it cannot be subjected to restrictive U.S. laws. On the Indian side however a number of things have to happen, including rationalizing the R&D establishment.[1] It has been stated that India's defence production establishments such as HAL are at least two to three decades behind in technology than their contemporaries in the West.

Public Private Partnership. The India has failed to develop a timely, transparent, and legitimate military procurement system or else defence

---

[1] A way forward in US-India defence cooperation. An interview with Dr Stephen P Cohen. www.brookings.edu/research/interviews/2011/07/us-indi-defense-cohen.dasgupta

procurement scam now discussed in the public domain would have not existed. The acquisition process has become highly bureaucratized, to the detriment of force capability and readiness. The introduction of private companies into the process may shake things up, although this is widely opposed for fear of corruption, the government's inability to enforce contracts against private parties, and secrecy.

"Strategic Autonomy" is what our Strategic thinkers prescribe for India. Under the present situation, U.S. will continue to balance China with India and use India to further its interest in Asia Pacific at a time when it plans to cut its own man power and have 'smart policies' to make up for defence cuts. We have examples of countries like the Pakistan, the Philippines to Great Britain and others that did not retain independent thinking on geopolitics and became dependant on the US military. Therefore, if India aspires to be a major international player it will have to do so on its own strength. But this does not mean that we take contradictory stand on geo-political issues but, what is best in the national interest in the long run.

India in Global Role. United States often accuses India of being vacillating and unreliable partner. The statement of Nicholas Burns, the former under secretary of State sums up, "Working with India is not easy, and some in Washington are impatient that it has, in some ways, failed to meet its obvious potential to lead globally. Our problem may not be an India that is too strong but one that is too weak and uncertain. Its diplomats have duelled with the United States unproductively on global trade talks and on other issues at the United Nations. It has stalled in implementing the nuclear deal with the United States and disappointed expectations it would open its economy further to foreign investment. It has not supported tough US and European sanctions against Iran and criticised NATO's successful intervention in Libya last spring." All may not be true but India positively dithers in decision taking which must be avoided.

Conclusion

Ushering of globalization and rise of terrorism with potential intersection with weapons of mass destruction, it became clear to U.S. government that it needed to combine forces with powerful emerging countries such as India (Brazil, Indonesia, and South Africa are others) to respond to these threats.

In this radically changed global environment, the basic interests of India and the United States, the world's largest and the world's oldest democracy have increasingly converged.

Current Indo- American ties are broad based and comprehensive. A relatively high level of joint military exercises, and naval cooperation and high level political and trade relations continue to take place between New Delhi and Washington's in contrast, the US Pakistan relations appear to be more focussed on war on terror and on countering nuclear proliferation. United States sees Pakistan as major source of Islamic radicalism. None the less, Pakistan till recently remained U.S. closest ally on war on terror because of its provision of considerable intelligence and logistical support to ISAF Afghanistan operations which now is beleaguered with problems due to the role of the terror outfits in Pakistan. One may ask what is there for United States in Indo-U.S defence relations. Actually the relationship is on quid pro quo basis. United States military's job during the Cold War was to deter Soviet expansionism. Today, it has identified Asia Pacific /East Asia and Indian Ocean as its focus areas. Describing the changed security perspective, U.S. Defence Secretary Leon Panetta asserted at the Shangri-La conference at Singapore on 02 Jun 2012, that U.S will expand its military power and presence in support of a deeper and more enduring partnership role in Asia-pacific region. In pursuance of this, U.S. will rebalance its Naval forces in the ratio of 60-40 between Pacific and Atlantic ocean by 2020. This change in strategic stance has become necessary for United States with the rise of Chinese power, while in contrast U.S. influence has declined in the Asia pacific. Moreover, the days of unilateralism are long over. Ever since U.S. military action in Iraq, the debate on unilateralism versus Multi-lateralism has also intensified. There is increasing realization in the world, including in the United States, that there is no alternative to multi-lateralism to prevent conflicts or for conflict resolution. The liberalists' concept of cooperative security has gathered momentum. This concept is founded on two arguments. First, new security challenges are diverse and multi-dimensional, such as terrorism, economic under-development, security of resources such as energy and water, illegal migrations, human rights abuses, piracy, drug trafficking and gun running, and environmental degradation. Second, the management of these issues cannot rely on unilateral or even bi-lateral measures but requires multi-lateral conflict prevention, peacekeeping and peace enforcement efforts. In this changed strategic environment, initiatives for cooperative security have to be taken by more powerful, stable and influential nations, particularly those having similar ideals and values. This is where the United States and Indian militaries have a tremendous potential for cooperation, at the regional and global levels. In this region, India is democratically and in most perspectives closer to United States hence, both could be reliable partners to further their interests. Of late, there has been discussion in the media on possible down gradation of India and U.S. defence relations after U.S. companies (Boeing / Lockheed) lost bid in MMRCA is not entirely true as Arms sale is only one component of evolving defence relations. The military to military interaction bellies this .India for example till last year carried out nearly sixty Joint exercises with United Sates in contrast to Russia with whom since 2003 only five joint exercises have been carried out. In fact, Russia was so much incensed after loosing the MMRCA contract that it cancelled two planned exercises last year. United States too was disappointed but, has refuted the impact of the failed deal. In fact, after recent India's Agni V missile test, US state departments spokesman stressed the strength of our defence ties saying "You Know we have got very strong strategic and security partnership with India".[2] Dr. Stephen P. Cohen the U.S. Defence Strategist suggests that,"over the years the United States and India has concluded several agreements or dialogues but there is has no mechanism for tracking progress in these areas in any transparent fashion. What the United States needs to do next is to identify, fund, and staff projects on one or two key technologies where actual cooperation can proceed pace rather than engage in a wide array of mostly token and ineffective dialogues".[3]

In new Delhi, in his last leg of nine days tour of Asia -Pacific region, Defence Secretary, Leon Panetta admitted that existing bottlenecks in Indo-US defence transactions essentially caused by bureaucratic hurdles in India and United States and defence procurement process of India which is still

---

[2] Hindu 20 Apr 2012

[3] A way forward in US-India defence cooperation. An interview with Dr Stephen P Cohen. www.brookings.edu/research/interviews/2011/07/us-indi-defense-cohen.dasgupta

evolving but, he assured that United States would initiate measures to facilitate unhindered technology access and sharing with India after India's Defence minister emphasised that priority for India was to move beyond the Buyer Seller transactions and focus on Transfer of Technologies(ToT) and partnerships to build indigenous capabilities.[4]

---

[4] The Hindu .7 Jun 2012. and MoD press release http://pib.nic.in/newsite/erelease.aspx?relid=84715

www.ingramcontent.com/pod-product-compliance
Lightning Source LLC
Chambersburg PA
CBHW070107100426
42743CB00012B/2668